SOLID AS A ROCK "I" STAND

Inspirational Poetry
&
Short Stories

SOLID AS A ROCK "I" STAND

Inspirational Poetry & Short Stories

by Luella Hill

Straight From The Heart Associates
P.O. Box 2208
Oakland, CA 94621

ISBN: 0-9640181-1-X (paperback)
"Solid As A Rock "I" Stand" Printed in 1998

Solid As A Rock "I" Stand
- Inspirational Poetry & Short Stories

Copyright © 1998 Luella Hill - Library of Congress.

Library of Congress Catalog Card Number: 97-92548.

All rights reserved. No part of this publication may be reproduced or transmitted in any form or by any means, electronic or mechanical, including photocopying, recording, or any information storage and retrieval system without permission in writing from Straight From The Heart Associates.

Straight From The Heart Associates
P.O. Box 2208, Oakland, California 94621

Printed in United States of America.

TABLE OF CONTENTS

Acknowledgements viii
About The Illustrator xi
About The Cover Designer xiii
About The Author xiv

Introduction by Danielle V. Laguerre 1
Dedication: Oh Sister 2

TODAY'S TROUBLE

Kidnapped Away From Freedom 6
Real 8
This and That 9
Last Tears 11
Purse Snatcher 12
Give Stress A Rest 14
On-A-Mission 15
Don't Cry 17
'Scuse Me 19
Counting Up The Losses 20

A LETTER & MEDITATION

Stay Free 24
A Question For You 27
Silent Calm 29

A THREE PART POEM

Wrong Place 32
White Dusty 33
Snatched By Crack 34

A LITTLE LIGHT STUFF

Bathroom Singer 36
Talker 38
Completeness 39
The Price of Love 40
Changes In The Weather 41
Counts 42

COURTING AND LOVE

My Chocolate Man 44
Past & Present Love 45
Mr. Interruption 46
Permitted Names 48
"Reasonable Expectation" 49

MORE THAN A BEDROOM IDENTITY

Bedroom Identity 52
Three-B Necessity 53
100% 55
Get-A-Job 56
WE 57
Sad Morning 59
It Hurts 61
One Thousand Times 63

FAMILY BATTLES

Black Man 66
Daddy 69

Daddy On A Cane 70
Come Back 72
Dark Scars 74
Attention, All Brothahs 75
Just-A-Penny 77
Divorce, of Course 78
Personal Benefits 80
The Day of Acceptance 81
Roses 82
Magic Man 83
Steps 84

The Creative and Clever Wit of Luella Hill

OLD-TIME RELIGION

Understanding 88
You Forgot 90
Who's In Charge 91
Master & Key 92
Fear 93
Bad Deal 94
Sleep-In-Peace 95
The Reward 96
When It's All Over 97
This Place Is Not My Home 98
No Matter What 99
God and Luella's Conversation 110

MESSAGE GRAMS 117

Biblical Reference 126

ACKNOWLEDGMENT I

HEAVENLY FATHER, I Stretch My Hands To Thee for I Want To Stand Solid As A Rock Thank you, God, For Being Real To Me Thank you, God, for being my Mother, Father, Friend, and Greatest Savior.

God, I give All My Best Praises To You
Thank you for planting the seed of poetry and inspiring words in my spirit, Thank you For The Bittersweet Times Of My Life, Thank you For Keeping Me Humble During The Storm As It Passed Over, Thank you For Accepting Me Into Your Presence.

God, I Thank You, Because When The Devil Tried To Make Me Feel that I Was Nothing or Nobody,
    You Proved him To Be A Liar Everytime
    You said if I put My Hand In Your Hand Then,
    <u>Solid As A Rock I Would Stand</u>
    And <u>now</u>, because you said:
    "I am more than a conqueror"
    I Can Look Ahead And Say
    Come on, storms; come on, trials;
    come on, tribulations!!!

ACKNOWLEDGMENT II

Professional Business Consultant
  - Dr. Rosie Milligan
Advisor - James Todd II, Ph.D.
Book Cover/Layout Designer - Gene Buban
Illustrator - Kelvin Curry
Editor - Ernestine Patterson

Encouragement Committee:

Danielle Laguerre, Esquire
Carolyn Davis
Lequita Dillon
April William
Lee Williams
family, and friends

AC Transit Drivers in the East Bay Area
Muni Driver in San Francisco, CA
samTrans Drivers in Daly City, CA
I am one passenger who appreciates you the
  most.

Most of all much love to the City of Oakland.

ACKNOWLEDGMENT III

Special thanks to the following booksellers:
Mr. Issac Taggart
Mrs. Janice Ross
Mrs. Penny Sanders
Ms. Tamiko Johnson
Mrs. Karen Johnson
Mrs. Blanche Richardson
Mr. Jerry Thompson
Mr. Shamba
Mr. Wadaddah & Family
Mr. Tim Daniel & Family
Mrs. Carol Mc Neal
Ms. Miriam Pollack and Mr. Robert Vaughters
Malik Bookstore
and Zahra's Books N' Things

Distributor: U.B. & U.S. Books & Things
           Khalifah

Al Galasso - President, Northern American Bookdealer Exchange

ABOUT THE ILLUSTRATION
KELVIN CURRY

"Whether art mirrors life or influences it may continue to be a cloudy issue for some, it's clear that the breadth, vibrancy, and accessibility of our cultural scene is due largely to the creative partnership between artists and community," says Oakland, California native Kelvin Curry.

After attending San Jose State University where he majored in Graphic Arts Design. Curry's drive toward cultivating such an alliance was unyielding, resulting in the creation of Black Concepts Gallery and collaborations with Laney College, Black Adoption Placement & Research Center. The Highland Foundation, and The Henry Robinson Multi-Service Center.

A famous writer once wrote, "change the world of a child and you change the world". These words were impetus for the popular Eyes of Tomorrow series, a creative mixture of pastel, watercolor, and pencil drawing, representing approximately 90% of Mr. Curry's work. The collection is truly a memento for those who cherish captivating moments in children's lives.

Creative energy is derived from the hope of enhancing the meaning of life through his artistry. The texture of the scope of his illustrations skillfully elicits contemplative, reminiscent, and joyful stimulus to this end.

Among the list of public displays are: Artisan Emporium Gallery, Ethnic Arts, Mosadi Gallery, Artists' Television Access State of the Art Gallery, Laney College and The National Institute of Arts and Disabilities (NIAD) gallery. Arts festivals include: The African Marketplace Cultural Festival, Festival at the Lake, The 13th Annual Pan-African Festival, Cleveland State University, Chase Western Reserve, and The 13th Annual National Convention of Black Mayors. Mr. Curry has also, participated in The Black Expo; Black History Celebration at PG & E, Fremont Public High School, The Western Addition Cultural Center, Genentech, Inc., and Los Angeles' eminent Artists Salute to Black History Month; Juneteenth Celebration in Berkeley, Richmond and San Jose. Noted jazz musician Wynton Marsalis and the musical group Tony, Toni, Tone' are among the many who own his work.

ABOUT THE COVER DESIGNER GENE BUBAN

Gene Buban, a.k.a Geneus, is truly a renaissance artist of the digital age. Mastering traditional art media such as pencils, charcoal, pastels, and acrylics, and even spray paint, Gene has brought his artistic skills to the computer where he endeavors to push the envelope in computer graphics in the realms of print, video, multi-media and the world wide web. His streetwise style captures the spirit and energy of today's youth with the goal of empowering and inspiring creativity through technology.

A graduate of the Computers in Art Special Major from San Jose State University, Gene has been involved in experimental computer graphics on the "bleeding edge." CypherDemensia was an interactive gallery exhibition combining full sized spray-painted graffiti murals with computer generated images which immersed the audience in the mural showing at SJSU and the Blasthaus gallery in San Francisco..

His videographics have appeared in international video publications such as VideoMaker, AmigaWorld, Video Toaster User, Videography, Digital Video, Camcorder, AVVideo/MultiMedia Producer.

He heads Neuroglyphic Communications, a high impact visual communications company in the San Francisco Bay Area. He can be reached via e-mail at geneus1@aol.com.

ABOUT THE AUTHOR

"Solid As A Rock "I" Stand by Luella Hill is her third published book of poetry. Her words are but a glimpse of a source, that flows from the heart of human consciousness. The power of words, as she calls it, are a collage of thoughts in effect tempered by the bitter and sweet dilemmas and dramas that are a path of the Black Experience in America.

Ms. Hill's collection was inspired by the deaths of her mother and sister which occurred seven months of each other. The adversities that have befallen Ms. Hill have been the seed to higher achievement.

Born in Madison County, Mississippi and abandoned by her mother at the age of three, she was placed in a foster home with an abusive alcoholic woman and lived as a battered child for five years. At the age of eight, her father gained custody of her and appointed her older sister as legal guardian.

Now living in California with her family, she kindled the sparks of her spiritual strength, and as she grew, renewed her trust in people. In the solitude of her writing, she found power and knowledge in her own words. Her experiences have given her an increased passion for human dignity, thus realizing her heart and consciousness are one. Ms. Hill is self-taught poet, whose poetry flow with smoothness of jazz and is contemporary as Hip-Hop. Her verses are keenly woven stanzas that set forth the metaphor in which she examines today's social pressures speaking straight from the heart of the Black Experience. Ms. Hill is the proud recipient of several awards including, 1994 Best Book of the Year Award in category of General Interest. Certificate of Recognition from International Black Writers and Artists, Inc., "Outstanding Poet Award by the City of Oakland, California presented by Mayor Elihu Harris and "The Editor's Choice Award by National Library of Poetry.

    Ms. Hill has been a featured poet for Alexander Book Company for The Rhythm River Poetry, Do 4 Self Enterprises for Poetic Elegance; A and Q's Nice Things; Martin Luther King Celebration at Naval Medical Center Oakland, International Black Writers and Artists, Inc., San Francisco African-American Historical & Cultural Society; Barnes & Nobles and for Mother's Hen poetry reading at Spasso Coffeehouse, and Inner City Ministries' Women's Department.

    Ms. Hill has been in Northern American Bookdealer Exchange magazine, The Sun Reporter, San Francisco Metro Reporter, NMCO Red Rover, New Poets Generation, and Oakland Tribune newspapers.

    Ms. Hill, a young ambitious black woman, struggling against the odds, is turning up on the winning side. She is expressing her affection for humanity and demonstrating there is power through words.

Solid As A Rock "I" Stand

INTRODUCTION

How often do we come across a young poet whose work questions the very nitty gritty some of us call life? She screams through her verses, and beats her poetic drum, til we hear her moving songs.

From prison bars, her hollow shrieks are heard, when she whips out her pen, to make the page DANCE.

>DANCE, SISTER, DANCE

To the White House, she sings her complaints, screaming for justice, in a world gone truly mad.

>SING, SISTER, SING

Chocolate sisters, melting softly in the heat. Brown brothers succumbing to the raw taste of forbidden sweets. LUELLA HILL knows no bounds, stops at no door, and obeys only one law: THE HEART AND SOUL OF HER POETRY!

Girl, when I curl up in bed with your work, I do enjoy the company!

>Danielle V. Laguerre, Esquire

Solid As A Rock "I" Stand

OH SISTER

Dedicated To: Rosie Lee Allina

You were the one appointed by God to be a mother to me. You were a gift heaven passed down to me.

OH SISTER

How times has past between the two of us the time that once was is no more in our lives everything else may have come and gone but I am right here with you to weather this storm.

OH SISTER

How I love you.

Forget about the many mistakes and the terrible, terrible heart aches still you are my sister.
You were only human to be human
is to error to make errors
one must forgive
in order to live
be at peace
my sister.

OH SISTER

You have stood the test of time
now you can live with a peace of mind

OH SISTER

The love you have for me
I had to stop to say thank you
for you sacrificed your life
to be a mother to me
when no one else wanted to be.

You clothed me; you kept food in my mouth;
and you provided well for me.

You are the special one
who was more than a sister;
a mother to a child
that you did not conceive
but still God had you in the plan;
you was the mother for me.

OH SISTER

Solid As A Rock "I" Stand

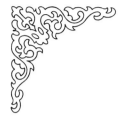

TODAY'S TROUBLE

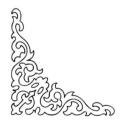
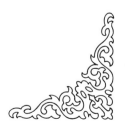

KIDNAPPED AWAY FROM FREEDOM

Security Gate at the front door
Security Gate at the back
three dead-lock bolts on every door
iron bars covering every window
security system, burglar alarm installed

> in the house
> at the job
> the corner grocery store
> the church-house

and another alarm ———— in the car

ALARM CITY

I'm not the criminal
I'm not armed, but I'm alarmed
Usually convicts are given sentences,
not law-abiding citizens.

No-one ever announced
      three-strikes-you're-out to me;
no judge sentenced me five to ten years
my reality is not automatic life sentence
without the possibility of parole.

Usually convicts are given sentences
not law-abiding citizens.

Solid As A Rock "I" Stand

my address is not San Quentin
        Santa Rita Prison
        Jamestown
        Fulsom State Prison
        Vacaville State Prison
        a local jail
    or any other correctional facility

But staring at all these bars
    that surround me
reminds me
    that I have been kidnapped
        away from freedom
My residence
    is where
        I'm supposed
            to be free

Solid As A Rock "I" Stand

REAL

Society has created so much independence between
        men
            and
                women

that togetherness now seems obsolete.

                Dial one nine-hundred: fake sex
                purchase climax for sale
           wishful thinking magazines
           toys for pleasure
    and you can rent tease-me tapes

Too much modernization
has stolen the more natural forms of love
But now,
you are not being charged $3.98 per minute
this is not a video
    I'm not in a magazine
      I'm not a computer game
        I'M REAL
          I'M IN YOUR FACE
            Touch Me!

Solid As A Rock "I" Stand

THIS AND THAT

    You tell me this;
    You tell me that;
but when I'm steppin' you ain't got my back!

You told me don't be concerned about those boys,
go in your room and play with some educational
toys.

    You tell me this;
    You tell me that;
but do you really got my back?

You tell me about going to school
to increase my skill not even knowing
how I feel.

You tell me, my foolish ways need to be put on hold;
sit down chile and let me preach about thinking of
goals.

    You tell me this;
    You tell me that;
but oh will you really have my back?

You tell me spending all my money and time looking
cute, is not success business suit.

    You tell me this;
    You tell me that;

Solid As A Rock "I" Stand

You tell me that my mind is what will save my dirty behind.

    You tell me this;
    You tell me that;
Mama why are you riding my back?

Mama says: I'm riding your back for you
    to not be surprised, that life is
        not a free ride.

Shakila: Okay, okay I'll try it your way.
    I'll sit down and
        think of a business choice
            so I don't have to
                constantly hear your voice.

        Two years later, I developed a
    product now it's on sale but
you ain't standing in line. Do
you know how I can tell?

You told me that you believe
    So I organized my own business
        so mama
            purchase my product for a dollar please.

LAST TEARS

"We are gathered here today
before this dearly beloved
    because he has broken the
        life covenant.

    Ashes to ashes, dust to dust
    into the final **Resurrection** of **CHRIST"**

How strange is it that even in the midst of a crowd I feel so alone in these pews because my best friend has died;

    Oh, so young to die.

The last tears of permanent good-bye are so painful like the beginning ache of a bout with the flu.

      GOOD-BYE
        GOOD-BYE

it is the sound of my heart that you may hear
    breaking
        from afar
            as the pall-bearers, roll-roll,
                then carry you away.

Solid As A Rock "I" Stand

PURSE-SNATCHER

Purse-Snatcher sneaked up so quick
and his moves was so slick
grabbed my purse with all my private things
pulling-pushing, this was no game
out of nowhere, smashed a blow to my face
this is a moment I can never erase.

Tussling me, almost to the ground
me holdin' on tight 'cause I ain't goin' down
scream-screaming loud and clear
tumbling in total fear.

The purse-snatcher's grip was so strong
but I was determined to hold on.

Where is the police, I'm thinking in my head
I hear no siren, nor see a light that's red
so, I let go before beaten till dead

Damn that purse-snatcher

Solid As A Rock "I" Stand

Solid As A Rock "I" Stand

GIVE STRESS A REST

Robbing somebody don't make you financially secure
    just stressed

choosing the wrong friends
    ain't the same as finding true friends;

      not knowing the difference causes stress

Often, being alone is better than being in with the wrong crowd
    this wisdom helps you avoid stress

about to lose your job don't mean you have to lose your mind
    because that would be double-stressed

    someone you know's living better than you
      don't mean your time will never come
        but you are still stressed

      can't wear the latest fashion;
    did you forget that the fashion-plate is
        you?
        so why stess?

PUT STRESS TO REST

Solid As A Rock "I" Stand

ON A MISSION

You are always complaining
you complain about my clothes
I never complained about how
you look being

ON A MISSION

You told me I was a bad
representation of you but
you never thought about
your representation of me being

ON A MISSION

You insulted my mentality
Never not once have I insulted
your mentality about being

ON A MISSION

You even broke into my mail box
stole my hard earned pay check
which forced me to walk to work

but "I" never not once complained
about being broke because of you being

ON A MISSION

Solid As A Rock "I" Stand

You sold our car for a nickel or dime
the thought of us was nowhere on your
mind being
          ON A MISSION

You lost a good paying job all
because of you being

          ON A MISSION

You even sold the babies'
toys, pampers, formula,
brand new school clothes,
and shoes all because of being

          ON A MISSION

You gave our furniture away but "I"
"I" never not once complained about
the house being empty while you
were
          ON A MISSION

Innocent lives are being destroyed
by people like you
          ON A MISSION

Solid As A Rock "I" Stand

DON'T CRY

Oh mama don't you weep
because your darling son has
turned to the street.

        The streets don't care
        I know it's not fair
        but he chose to go out there.

Your son's so high because of
his choice, he can't even hear
the fear in the sound of your
voice.

        I know your son is doing dope
        saying this is the way
        he knows how to cope.

God is right there
He knows how much you care.
You done your best
now your son has to do the rest.

        Oh mama don't you weep
        because your darling son
        has turned to the street.

Solid As A Rock "I" Stand

Solid As A Rock "I" Stand

'SCUSE ME

'Scuse me can I borrow a dollar?
Spare change?

'Scuse me, mamma gotta a quarter
for uh cup of coffee?

'Scuse me, my brothah,
can you help a poor brothah out?

Come on!

Just a quarter, nickel, or even a dime

Looking him directly in his eyes
responding look my brothah, I wish
I could give you a quarter, nickel or
even a dime

But my brothah I won't make a
contribution to helping you lose your mind
now excuse me my brothah.

SPECIAL NOTE: This poem is for those who use homelessness as a scam.

Solid As A Rock "I" Stand

COUNTING UP LOSSES

Sitting in the San Francisco General Hospital,
Emergency Room Lobby, covered with shame, trying
to convince the police and myself that he isn't to
blame;

Where is he?

Running the street;
today, it's a black eye and a swollen cheek.

> Last week, it was a miscarriage,
> three weeks ago, a dislocated jaw.

A month ago,
ambulance rushed me to Highland Hospital
with a head concussion

> five weeks ago, fractured ribs

> six weeks ago, sexual abuse

what kind of love is this?

And there was the time I'd lost a baby who had been

POUND

out of me

Solid As A Rock "I" Stand

I thought there was so much love
but now I can only see the losses;

                lost dreams
                lost dignity
                lost respect

all in the name of love
or is it/<u>was</u> it
only in the name of him

Solid As A Rock "I" Stand

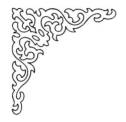

A
LETTER
&
MEDITATION

Solid As A Rock "I" Stand

STAY FREE

Dear Son,

I sit here in this cell,
wondering if you are doing well.

My love for you grows deeper everyday;
doing time will never make it fade away.

Jail is the zone known
as the criminal's home,
where you are truly on your own.
I am fighting to stay alive,
and keeping people off my hide.

No matter how good a player you are at any game;
somebody's got your number, and many have got
your name.

Such boring scenery, these prison bars,
can't trust your block mates or prison guards.

My wings have been clipped like a bird in a cage; one
time I was hip, now I'm filled with rage.

Son, I really wish I could be there for you,

But...

Solid As A Rock "I" Stand

Solid As A Rock "I" Stand

It is my own fault I am a prisoner;
My crimes are mine and mine alone;
If even you commit a crime;
you will serve some time.

Let your life go on and be very strong
daddy's love grows deeper for you everyday.

Little man be strong until daddy comes home.

Hoping, my son, you'll try to stay free;
you doing that will be my victory.
Be the man I failed to be—
Don't be the man who is me.

    Love,

    Daddy

II
A QUESTION FOR YOU

Are all crimes really wrong
when society makes it necessary
              enticing?

We hear that Charity Begins At Home;
but with the United States,
it begins across the sea.

In the United States, that's US, we find

      people getting laid off daily
         a scarce job market
    a cost of living which constantly increases
        a deliberate tearing apart of families
  an education system on the downfall
        computers and modern technology
  replacing people

This means that the only way that some have is
survival from the streets.

If you commit a crime
    which pays you
        one hundred dollars an hour,
you can't expect that honesty
    which gives you $5.25 an hour
        to logically win when rent

Solid As A Rock "I" Stand

food
clothing
and doctor bills are due

Is it the people who should be locked up
or the system which should be closed down?

Solid As A Rock "I" Stand

SILENCE CALM

Silent calm, silence, speak
closing the door that made me feel weak.

Silent calm, silence, speak
feeling the cold water that chills my feet

Silent calm, silence, speak
refreshing, cold water hidden
beneath my feet

Silent calm, silence, speak
asking the Lord for good news this week

Silent calm, silence, speak
looking at your curving waves
splashing my feet

Silent calm, silence, speak
my soul is restored from the quietness
the ocean speaks

Solid As A Rock "I" Stand

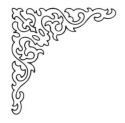

A THREE PART POEM

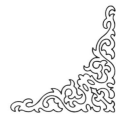

Solid As A Rock "I" Stand

WRONG PLACE

I.

PIPE CITY

You're now entering <u>Pipe City</u>
and it isn't very pretty.

Brothers and sisters so filled with smoke
smell is so awful, I just want to choke.
Some of us get so high and smoked up
till our minds and bodies are completely tore up;
bodies scare-crow thin, no life in the eyes when I
look at you, I instantly want to cry.

What will shake you up
so you can wake up and return to your original life
scene —> Drug Free

Solid As A Rock "I" Stand

II.

WHITE DUSTY

Sniffing that nickel
      sniffing that dime
      why sniff drugs that destroy your mind?

bent all over in just your bra
      sniffing cocaine through a straw
sniffing up the carpet
      face all blue

White Dusty captured another hostage, you see
for you cannot walk away and proclaim to be free

sniffing that nickel
      sniffing that dime
           sniffing up all your money
end result: destroyed your mind.

A mind is worth more than a nickel,
worth more than a dime,
hanging in there, believing things get better in time,

say no to White Dusty, you see,
for a natural high is the best, and it's free
sniffing White Dusty takes you to Jail
while your inner precious self slides downhill;
sniffing White Dusty is a death petition which only
prepares you for the mortician.

Solid As A Rock "I" Stand

III.

SNATCHED BY CRACK

Some people warned us we'd be hubba-heads; but we just ignored what they said.

Snatched By Crack in the palm of our hand; since then, our lives have been sinking quick-sand.

First, looking high, then looking low
for that cocaine white snow.

Smoking that crack has stolen our pride,
making us prisoners in-and-out-side;
and this is the reason, we sit in the
corner and cry.

It's crack living rent-free in our heads
let's pray we don't do this until we're dead.

LET'S SNATCH BACK FROM CRACK!!

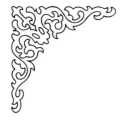

A LITTLE LIGHT STUFF

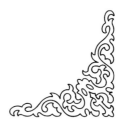

Solid As A Rock "I" Stand

BATHROOM SINGER

Bathroom Singer is who I am;
Bathroom is my place to jam.

        Bathroom walls are where I get down;
    Don't have to worry about how bad I sound.

Bathroom singing is how I groove
the bathroom is where I set the mood.

        Yes, I know, it's my Hollywood zone,
    so what! If front stage is really my home!

Bathroom Singer I begin to sing loud
Neighbors are stomping and screaming saying:
"SHUTTUP! child

        Finally, time to step from the shower
    that was such fun: my singing voice hour!

Bathroom Singer that's who I am
A bathroom is the place to jam

        Sometimes I think I might be flat;
    But you don't think I care about that!

Here, in my voice's secret place,
I get to sing a little and wash my face.

Solid As A Rock "I" Stand

Bathroom singing: this is how I get free;
the audience and super-star are,
guess who! **ME!**

Because **I AM THE BATHROOM SINGER**

TALKER

Although he is not alone
this conversation with no-one in particular
keeps going on and on
the passengers look around and
listen intently.

Those who talk to themselves often get more
attention than those who talk with someone else.

Do you think the talker is crazy?

Solid As A Rock "I" Stand

COMPLETENESS

Life is a puzzle with millions of pieces,

never complete until the final part is in

place.

Today, I will collect my pieces,

and tomorrow, you will gather yours;

then, together,

we will fit them into one another

to see the beautiful life we shared

Solid As A Rock "I" Stand

THE PRICE OF LOVE

The price of love doesn't come with a fee;

All you have to do is appreciate me.

The price of love means letting me be free;
then, you can be you; and I can be me.

Always knowing that you are there,

And that , in the hard times, you will still care —that is my price of love.

Solid As A Rock "I" Stand

CHANGES IN THE WEATHER

Sunshine enlivens me;

Clouds depress me;

Storms scare me;

Earthquakes make me feel that

God is upset;

Tornadoes make me want to run;

but I can't hide from God;

What do you think I should do?

COUNTS

As life's situations unfolded,
    I began to feel popular
        When I counted my friends.

But, really,
    my popularity diminished
        when my success was finished.

I discovered that those who were my true friends
were the ones who were there till the bitter end.

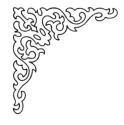

COURTING AND LOVE

Solid As A Rock "I" Stand

MY CHOCOLATE MAN

(In my mind, I am visualizing My Chocolate Man)

My chocolate-brown man is so rich and sweet, from his gorgeous head to his precious feet.

His soul and spirit are full of pride
which can't be bargained with or pushed aside.

He accepts and gives unconditional love
making life on earth like heaven above.

Let Cupid guide him by the hand,
leading him to where I stand;
and here I stand at this very tree,
wondering if he'll ever find me.

They say good things come to those who wait; but waiting so long makes me question fate and ask:

Where, where is My Chocolate Man?

Solid As A Rock "I" Stand

PAST AND PRESENT LOVE

January:	I loved Tyrone
April:	I loved Antione
August:	I loved Ricky
December:	I loved Steven

I spoke to God everytime I fell in love. I sometimes thought God wonder why my child loved a different man every quarter.

My reply to Him was
   Father gotta have me some:

Summer:	Love
Winter:	Love
Spring:	Love
Fall:	Love

Cause all the time I knew I had your Heavenly love.

Solid As A Rock "I" Stand

MR. INTERRUPTION

Walkin' down the street in ma sun-dress
on a hot summer night

I soon hear one man say:

>"baby you so f-i-i-i-i-ne I could
tear that dress up! Are you tired, baby?
You should be, 'cause girl, you been running
across my mind all day."

Another one says:

>"Where's yo' man at? If I was
him, I couldn't let nothing this
fine be walkin' the streets
>
>Yo' name should be cookies,
because you'd crumble in ma
arms."

And would you <u>believe</u> another one says:

>"Hey, hey, girl! Come over
here! I ain't gon bite! I just wanna nibble."

And no! That wasn't enough;
somebody else says:

Solid As A Rock "I" Stand

> "You got a man? How long
> you HAD that problem?"

They don't know that they done tore they pants with me, so I say:
Mr. Interruption!

My **problem**
      just appeared
           when **I heard your approach**

TO THE WOMAN OF THE YEAR!"

Solid As A Rock "I" Stand

PERMITTED NAMES

Women should never respond
>to negative names;

>not to bitch,
>>because that's a female dog;

>not to whore,
>>because you might be mistaken

>>>and besides,
>>>>it took a man
>>>>to make her that way

Speak my birth-name with dignity;

>Speak my name with honey on your tongue
>and sugar in your heart.

Then, I **can** answer you
>for **then**
>>I did hear you call my name

Solid As A Rock "I" Stand

"REASONABLE EXPECTATION"

She must be f-i-i-i-ine
she must be equipped with a good,
solid job
                      bad crib
she must know how to make love
        know how to cook up a storm
and lord, you know, she got to be clean
and she cain't have no cryin' kids
and, of course, got to worship me like a king.

I will fulfill your expectations
if I could get more from you than expectations.

**Have you stopped to think
what I expect from you?**

Solid As A Rock "I" Stand

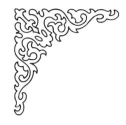

MORE THAN A BEDROOM IDENTITY

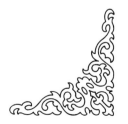

Solid As A Rock "I" Stand

1
MORE THAN A
BEDROOM IDENTITY

It's amazing how so many men brag about their
greatness in bed but you never see their performance
outside the bedroom;

Oh, such sweetly-spoken words,
building toward the ecstasy I've longed for riding the
tides so smoothly,

steering me
      stirring me
like a boat through the waters of passion,
      never at a loss,
always in control
      ready to conquer all in the bedroom.

Somehow, though, the day-to-day living of a
successful love affair is an impossible challenge.

So I've made up a new rule:

No entry to my bedroom
      until you have properly identified yourself
          as a man
              outside my bedroom door

II

THREE -B NECESSITY

For that, I think I need a three-B Man
I got to have three-B Necessity
I need you to be steppin' behind me
to be chillin' beside me
and through the rough times
to standin' behind me
BE HERE!

Solid As A Rock "I" Stand

Solid As A Rock "I" Stand

III
100%

They say ninety-nine and a half won't do!
Gotta have one hundred percent
when it's me and you:

one-hundred percent in loyalty
    affection
        mutual commitment

    one-hundred percent in
        providing for and
            helping each other

            taking care of one
        another's babies

    enduring to the
end.

They say ninety-nine and a half won't do!

        That's why I
got to have one hundred percent when it's
        me and you.

Solid As A Rock "I" Stand

GET A JOB

Oh, my God, I want my man to
get a job.

I guess he's totally allergic to the thought
it seems unreal to him.

He walks around like our love could
pay our bills:

he say:

> "Baby, I am tryin' but, you know
> the white man always keeps a
> <u>Brother</u> down". But this is it

I look at him in a scream

**"The only white man that's keepin' YOU down
is my WHITE bedroom sheets.**
That is the only street where we're willing to meet!

Hey! honey
    Sugar-plum
        Get A Job

Solid As A Rock "I" Stand

WE

Oh, no honey you did not mean
the word "WE"

because WE, Women, know about and hate the
improper usage of this word

WE

I'm your honey
    your sugar
    your baby
    your girl

I'm your wanna be
      gunna be
      wife

But, basically, I'm none of the above
because WE only need my money.

From what I know, the word "WE"
goes along with the word "US"

But the truth is
that it's just Me,
not WE.

Solid As A Rock "I" Stand

WE ain't printed on My pay-check;
WE ain't there when the bills show up in
 My name;
WE ain't shared not one damned expense
 to help cover my life;
WE ain't calling Me to show that <u>we</u> care;
WE ain't concerned about my needs;
WE ain't never there,
 ain't nowhere to be found
 when I'm constantly alone.

 I'm your wanna be
  gunna be
  wife?

WE = Us, which we never was;
WE = Togetherness, but on what do we agree?
WE = Commitment, but you don't understand
 <u>Loyalty</u>
WE = Unity, but <u>we</u> were never one (1);
WE = two people, which is all we'll ever be.

SAD MORNING

It's a sad morning,
when tears, streaming down my cheeks,
make me realize I must miss my sunrise treat.

It's a sad morning,
being absent from the arms that energized me;

Today, I am lonely;
Yesterday, that was my partna to play.

Now, instead of lying in his arms,
the only arms that I feel are my own
because he has taken his love and moved on.

It's a sad morning,
spending my time, stroking the sheets
remembering the good, strong motion imprinted on my mind.

Oh, it's a sad morning,
missing yo' good thang,

'cause yo man done los' the common-sense of Us in his brain

Oh, it's a sad morning
shedding tears because I have been evicted from his heart

Solid As A Rock "I" Stand

Even though, everyday,
I was thinking that my strivings
were fulfilling my part

OH, WHAT A SAD MORNING!

Solid As A Rock "I" Stand

IT HURTS

It Hurts

>the amount of time I wasted
>being with you

It Hurts

>my devoted love kept me going
>strong during the
>crazy motion love
>is blind, so I couldn't see the harm

It Hurts

>knowing I made the wrong choice to
>stand by someone who didn't stand by me

It Hurts

>knowing that during the time of my needs
>you became deaf and did not hear my plead

It Hurts

>I felt that I was sometimes too good
>and in other ways, not good enough
>in your sight

Solid As A Rock "I" Stand

A true lover understands my needs as well as his own.

True love must be handled like a priority,
not an over-sight;
there has to be something greater
than the misery
I found in you

                    IT HURTS
                    IT HURTS
                    IT HURTS!

Solid As A Rock "I" Stand

ONE THOUSAND TIMES

WOMEN are HURT OVER ONE THOUSAND TIMES A DAY.

But

        disappointment

        deception

        dishonesty

        abandonment

        and broken commitments

have made some women what they are today

STRONG

Solid As A Rock "I" Stand

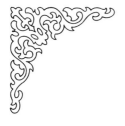

FAMILY BATTLES

Solid As A Rock "I" Stand

BLACK MAN

It seems
    that a Black Man
        only knows peace
            in the womb;

After he is born,
    he is turned into a fighter,
        steadily caught in the ring of life.

The Black Man's gym is his mind.
    He fights,
        not against flesh,
            but against a power
                that's well-defined.
He is the mat
    constantly stepped on;

His opponent throws a jab at his pride
    an upper-cut to his dignity
        a strong right to his finances
            a kidney-punch to his dream of
        a united family.

    When a Black man becomes tired
        of being a punching bag
            he leans back a little
                just
                    to
                        relax

Solid As A Rock "I" Stand

Suddenly, he comes back swinging
>**knock-outs!**
>>**knock-outs** against ignorance
>**knock-outs** for his self respect.

This is better
>than going in the corner
>>to restore his lacerated dignity
>>>and to sober-up
>>from his punch-drunk pride.
><u>FIGHT</u> on, <u>BLACK</u> fighter;
because,
>he who fights can tell a good story,
>>and he who does not,
>>>wins no glory!

Solid As A Rock "I" Stand

Solid As A Rock "I" Stand

DADDY

I was quiet as a little mouse
when Daddy came staggering into the house.

Daddy was drunk from what I could tell,
and so he did not look very well.

There must have been another fight
because he left mama again tonight.

He slammed shut, banged the door,
saying he would not tolerate this mess anymore

Daddy spun off into the night in a spin;
All I seen was a cloud of wind.

It was clear that my daddy was really upset;
these are the moments I'll never forget.

Solid As A Rock "I" Stand

DADDY ON A CANE

Old Daddy On A Cane
pimpin' and limpin' with the youngstas gang games;
    watching him droolin' while
    sistahs walking by;
they could rock his world right away.
Now he's whistling and moving his hand
    trying to flirt
as the young sisters walk by in their tight mini skirts.

Knowing his heart is about to clasp
times like this is zap! Old Daddy On A Cane
look to be around seventy or eighty
out here chasing baby.

Look at him chillin' in his red caddy;
blowing' his horn, honking like pimp daddy.

Daddy Cane layin' that drama so thick
he's about to get into the mix.

Ms. Young Thang is collecting his money
    like bees on honey
and in their own mind this must be funny.

Older men was the original teachers to young
children to doing the right thang.

Crossing my legs as I lean against this building,
thinking well old daddy cane

Solid As A Rock "I" Stand

I'm gonna chill with my forty ounce brew but don't forget some young brotha got they eye on you.

Daddy Cane
      young brothah's would have
           probably listened
                to what you have to say
          if you wasn't to busy
    chillin with young honeys just to lay.

Two wrongs can't speak about a right. I'll keep on chillin on the corner
      drinking my forty ounce brew
           'cause Old Daddy On A Cane
                has lost hope too.

COME BACK

Mama may not be a perfect angel
'cause she left me here with these
total strangers.

My heart screams and cries out to you
      mama I really do not know what to do
mama you are my line of protection
      in this life of mine with no direction.

You are the one who holds the key
      without you, my identity is a mystery.

Here my tears flows like a river
      mama I was never looking for gold nor silver.

Mama I stretch my hands out to you
      wanting to touch you and hold you too

To leave me mama means you also
      left yourself
            I am apart of you

WE ARE ONE
COME BACK

Solid As A Rock "I" Stand

Solid As A Rock "I" Stand

DARK SCARS

Dark scars
    on my little heart
        for my mother;
            the pain is as great as the fear.

I don't know my sisters or brothers;
    their voices I'm longing to hear.

But crawling in life each day
    has made me wonder and say—

    if they were to ever see me,
        would they snicker:
            "Just go away".

Solid As A Rock "I" Stand

ATTENTION, ALL BROTHAH'S

Attention: All brothahs report to the deck!
Attention: All brothahs report to the deck!

Not to the deck of cards to play
      gin rummy with the fellas
      spades or strip poker with the wrong one

no brothahs this is a call for you to return
from the deck you walked away from

HOME

The deck where only you are the captain
who controls his ship

HOME

When the captain slips away all aboard
his ship will sink and pass away

Attention: All brothahs report to the deck!
Attention: All brothahs report to the deck!

A captain is not just a rank.
      You are a captain without enlisting in
      Uncle Sam's Army.

You are a captain without a uniform
worn for his country. There's a uniform
you wear before your family

Solid As A Rock "I" Stand

CAPTAIN OR MAN

The captain has authority
as a man has authority in his family

When the captain abandons the ship
leaving the family not equipped

How do we survive?

Attention: All brothahs report to the deck!
Attention: All brothahs report to the deck!

We need the captain onboard to make sure the anchor is cast properly to shore,
watching fathers walking through home door, and taking their place inside front door.

Saving the drifting and dying families
who were leaving shore; teaching your children families' values can be restored

DESPERATE FOR THE CAPTAIN

All brothahs attention on the deck!
All brothahs pay attention off the deck!

WE NEED YOU

Solid As A Rock "I" Stand

JUST A PENNY

Grandma always said: "Pennies make dollars."

I walk down the street
      find a penny here
             and a penny there
walk two blocks further and find three pennies
clustered together

I walked into the cafe;
      there's a penny on the floor
          I turn and walk back
              a penny is even at the door.

Suddenly, I think: "this is my lucky day."
so many pennies, but no thoughts to be found.
What happened to all the thoughts that go with these
pennies?

Is it really my lucky day
        or is it a thought I never heard
              for just a penny?

DIVORCE, OF COURSE

Divorce,
> of course,
>> is a final separation from something
we thought was a beautiful sensation.

Divorce,
> of course,
>> is full of stress;
so put on your boots to wade through mess.

DIVORCE

> a solution of the end the steady
> noise and confusion

DIVORCE

> a consequence of the choice to end
> that forever disagreeing voice

DIVORCE

> sometimes means half-and-half
> and at other times, waiting to see
> who has the last laugh.

DIVORCE

> an end of the old world, and a
> beginning of the new

Solid As A Rock "I" Stand

<u>BUT MOST OF ALL</u>

DIVORCE

      means a chance to live, baby
      totally without you.

PERSONAL BENEFITS

I will walk
    through fire and rain
        just to keep up with you;
When you're down, I'll be around,
There's no limit to what I'd do.

I will wipe every tear
    that falls from your eyes
        and replace it with a smile.

I will be your helping hand
    when you cannot tolerate anymore.

I will be your friend, until the very end.

Every step I make,
    I will do my best
        to represent you.

In return, what will be the benefits I receive?

Solid As A Rock "I" Stand

DAY OF ACCEPTANCE

Remember honey there is no
word like "I" nor you
the Day of Acceptance created a new
word called "WE".

When they gave me:

yo freedom
yo job
yo home
yo car
authority
opportunities
money
and respect

I collected it all for you
to make a stronger "WE".

Solid As A Rock "I" Stand

ROSES

I wish
roses would never die
for it gives me so much joy
inside
I smelled a rose today
that reminded me
of you in every way. The sweetness that
I smelled made me simply want to melt
for it was your love I instantly felt.

I smelled
a rose
today
and
deep
down
inside
I knew
once
again
your
love
saved
my
day.

Solid As A Rock "I" Stand

MAGIC MAN

Magicians can pull
              a rabbit from a hat;
But you, my baby,
              did far more than that.

You pulled more love,
              such love out of me,
that I didn't know I had,
              was afraid to see.

This is why a man
              with such love
should be handled
              with golden-soft gloves.

Solid As A Rock "I" Stand

STEPS

You can step in
    you can step out
        you can step up
            you can step down.

                    step mama
              step daddy
           step sister
        step brother.

There's no place where steps should be
'cause the bottom line is
we're straight up family —
no matter what steps it took to make us.

So let it be known
that the only steps I have to show
are the **entrance** and **exit** steps
to my world/door

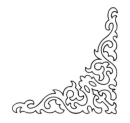

THE CREATIVE AND CLEVER WIT OF LUELLA HILL

Solid As A Rock "I" Stand

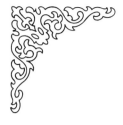 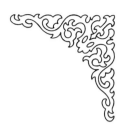

OLD-TIME RELIGION

Solid As A Rock "I" Stand

UNDERSTANDING

Assemblies Churches
Bahai Churches
Baptist Churches
Buddhist Churches
Catholic, Liberal Churches
Charismatic Churches
Christian Churches
Episcopal
Christian & Missionary Alliance
Christian Reformed
Christian Science
Church of Christ
Church of Christ Holiness
Church of God
Church of God In Christ
Church of God of Prophecy
Church of God 7th Day
The Later-Day Saints
Community Churches
Convenant Churches
Ecumenical Churches
Episcopal Church
Evangelical Churches
Foursquare Gospel
Full Gospel
Gnostic
Hebrew Christian
Independent Bible
Interdenominational
Japanese Christian

Solid As A Rock "I" Stand

Jehovah's Churches
Krishna Consciousness
Lutheran Churches
Mormon
Moslem Mosque
Nazarene
New Age
New Testament
Non-Denominational
Open Bible
Orthodox Eastern
Pentecostal Church of God
Presbyterian Church
Seventh-Day Adventist
Swendenborgian
Taoism
Unitarian Universalistic
Vedanta

Some people's religious beliefs often create confusion. I dream of all these religions focusing on that one God that the Gospel according to John chapter 1 verse 1 states "In the beginning was the word and the word was with God and the word was God".

Then there will never be debates on who's right about God.

God is Right All By Himself.

Solid As A Rock "I" Stand

YOU FORGOT

The minute you got up, you put me down;
now you are too good;

you forgot
     where you stood;

you forgot
     who helped you weather
     the storm;

you forgot
     I was the one who kept you warm;

You forgot
     I sacrificed my time

what do I get for not asking for a dime.

You forgot
     I'm the one who deserves
     the honor and respect

You forgot!

Solid As A Rock "I" Stand

WHO'S IN CHARGE

Never worry about the Devil breaking you down; for God lifts you up, when your spirit is tired and going round and round.

God speaks with authority,

saying:

> "YOU ARE MORE POWERFUL
> THAN THAT WHICH FIGHTS
> AGAINST YOU."

he says:

> "I COMMAND MY ANGEL
> TO SPREAD OPEN HIS WINGS
>
> ANGEL! POUR OUT YOUR SPIRIT!
>
> **ANGEL!** fight back on my child's behalf."

God now smiles on you and says:

> "IT IS NOW WITH JOY
> THAT YOU REMEMBER
> WHO'S IN CHARGE".

Solid As A Rock "I" Stand

MASTER & KEY

The devil enters God's parking lot
to test drive God's vehicles.

God said what keys would you like today;
look at Mister or Misses Alexis
>   BMW
>   Volvo
>   Toyota
>   Honda
>   Nissan
>   Ford
>   Cadillac
>   or the stretch limousine
>   or Roll Royce

Satan I have many more, look around
Satan thinking silently it's not the vehicle
I'm looking at my eyes is on the driver and
I want to be a passenger for the test drive.

God has much faith in his drivers, so he gave Satan
the keys because He knew his driver would make
Him pleased. I am God the Master and the Key, my
people know they can trust me.

Solid As A Rock "I" Stand

FEAR

Fear tried to get ahold on me today;
But fear, I'm sure,
     never stared me directly in the face
else it would have seen
     that I am wrapped in Divine Grace.

Fear may be mighty; but in God's arms
I'm wrapped to be strong,

Fear will not tremble me,
     even if people cast many stones.

Fear is a challenge to me, so I can display God's
victory; and I **know** everyday I got victory;

Victory is a promise,
even though I don't always feel it;
I simply name it and claim it, then victory appears.

Come here, fear, I am your testing ground;
Come with your best, because I am covered by God's
power that is written in and on my chest;

Fear knocked me to my knees.
But my knees are my meeting-place for talking
between God and me;

Yeah, fear, you have no place;
Yeah, fear, in my life, for you there is no space.

Solid As A Rock "I" Stand

BAD DEAL

The cards are being shuffled
the dealer passes the deck;
glancing at my hand, tells me that
I don't have a chance.

Looking at these cards, which are exactly like my life,
I want to scream:

"Missed deal. Misdeal!
Let me throw away this hand!
Let me throw in this hand!"
Misdeal!

Suddenly the dealer speaks to me
when no-one else is paying attention.

He say softly: I know you don't have any
     kings
          queens
              aces or
                  jacks

but, remember, I've got your back
Don't get caught up in the cards
     you see in your sight;
          Believe in me with all your might!"

I won!

Guess who the dealer was!

SLEEP-IN-PEACE

Sleep-In-Peace
Don't have to slumber
                nor live on snooze
for now you are onboard
                God's peaceful cruise.

Sleep on young or old soldier
      until God speaks
           to them young or old bones.
You are free from people casting stones.

Take your nap
            from this evil filled world
come on home old or young soldier
it's time to rest.

Take off your armor,
      remove your vest,
           pass on your sword of God,
                lay down your shield

Death collects like all other bills
sleep on
      young
          or older soldier

THE REWARD

The reward of salvation is great
for those who hold on to their faith
    then you will surely win
    and be able to get in
        to the gates of heaven.

I'll have my own key.
At this time my life will have gained the victory.
For our Heavenly Father will remember me.
    My armor may weigh me
    down but I'll steady keep on runnin'
        to achieve my crown.

Solid As A Rock "I" Stand

WHEN IT'S ALL OVER

When It's All Over
I want to lay on God's shoulder
and be finished with this on earth mess.

                         No more robberies
        killing
                inflation
      politics
                starvation
        homelessness
            racism
                      favoritism

no more bills
     hospitals

                no more recession
                      depression
            loneliness
                      broken-heartedness

no more let-downs
and best of all
no more work

I'll be glad when I'm able to lay on
God's shoulder.

Solid As A Rock "I" Stand

THIS PLACE
IS NOT
MY HOME

Mama:

Since you've been gone, this place is not my home.
Now it's just a stepping stone.

I'll know I finally made it on home when I
sit with you on God's throne.

There are so many things constantly wrong, that's
why I know it's not my home.

    Whenever I'm happy, safe, soft as foam,
then I'll know that's were I belong.

This is only part of a path by which I must
return;
because Oh no! This Place could not Possibly be my
home.

Solid As A Rock "I" Stand

NO MATTER WHAT

A PAINFUL ROAD TO CHRIST

A STORY OF FAITH

A neatly-dressed woman of about thirty or so stands at the entrance of her well-kept home. One can tell by the way she slams the door and sits on the front porch steps that she is upset. She is speaking to herself.

I loved this man who treated me wrong, I loved him no matter what. In my heart, I knew he didn't love me as much as I loved him, but I thought he would change if we stayed together, so I held on. I cooked full-course meals for him and kept the house clean.

I loved him when he had no money. When that happened, I paid all the bills and kept his gas-tank on full, so he could go riding with his friends. Yes, I even loved him when his so-called friends were his top priority.

When he was never there, I loved him. When he was cuddling someone else, and when it was over—I took him back and forgave him—and he didn't always have to beg.

Solid As A Rock "I" Stand

And now, look at me. He's got me feeling sorry for myself, feeling blue. My head's hangin' down. That's why I stepped out for a breath of fresh air, hoping I could clear my head. I don't feel like a woman anymore, because he doesn't need me. You got it! I love that man no matter how badly he treated me—I loved that man, no matter <u>what!</u>.

An old woman approaches the front steps. She is between sixty or seventy, carries a good-sized hand bag, and walks with dignity on a cane. The eyes of the two women meet. The old woman begins to speak.

Chile, what's troublin' you? You got angry written all over your face.

The younger woman says:

I've just discovered that for five years, I've been in love with someone who doesn't love me.

After telling her story, the elder replies. Love is a beautiful thing. It ain't all this foolishness and games. Maybe what you've got is the shadow and not the substance. Maybe what you got was an imitation of love and not the genuine love. People can paint a picture of **love** on a canvas. But **love** ain't a painting. Just because you feel a tinglin' in your heart, that don't mean you're in love. That tinglin' just means you're alive. Can I sit down with you for a moment?

Solid As A Rock "I" Stand

        The young woman nods, and
    beckons to the elder to share
her porch-step.

Sorry, I forgot my manners.

      The old woman says:

Let me introduce you to a man who's more than a one-night stand— who's been attracted to you all the time; a man who will meet all your needs before you ask him.

This man is a good man, an excellent provider: he won't abandon his woman. He is so proud of you. He will make you happy everyday you open your eyes. He will make you so secure, you'll never have to worry again. When you get this man into your life, you won't have to compete against any other woman, because he'll treat you with the utmost respect. He'll love you, no matter what—even when you don't love him. He loves you day-in-and-day-out—that's unconditional love! He won't every put you down, because His job is to lift you up, to make you smile.

At the thought of such a man, the younger woman smiles.

    Her heart beats faster with anticipation; she feels new life surging through her body.

The younger woman says:

who is this man, and where is he? If he loves me, why hasn't he told me, himself? You're sure he's still attracted to me? He must have been watching me all the time.

The younger woman asks:

Does this man have a job? If he's going to be that nice to me, I wouldn't care if he worked at McDonald's. Is it too late to meet him and where does he live—that's what I want to know? Are you sure this man likes me? After all, you, ... you really don't know me.

The old woman clears her throat, say: I know I don't know you. But child he knows both of us. And yes, he did say it was you that he liked. There's only <u>one</u> you, and he knows you very well.

Wait a minute—

But the younger woman interrupts

What about my man—the one I'm with.

The older woman looks deeply into the younger woman's eyes with compassion and speaks. What man?

Solid As A Rock "I" Stand

When I walked by here, I didn't see no man tryin' to console you for the hurts he's done to you. That's what <u>real</u> men are suppose to do. And to top if off, this man will even protect you from danger.

What man! What man!

    The younger woman gestures impatiently what's his name? Is he a celebrity?

    The older woman speaks.

Calm down; calm down. Wait a minute ... hold my cane while I pull up my slip ..., now, that's better. That's so embarrassing!

Well, he isn't really a celebrity. But he's known world-wide. He wrote a love-letter to you. Where's that love-letter—let me see if I can find it! It's in my purse.

The younger woman still impressed:

He wrote a love-letter to <u>me</u>! How long have you had it? The old woman pauses, and look reflectively at the older woman.

Can I ask you some question?

    The younger woman returns some of the anger to her face.

Solid As A Rock "I" Stand

You just playin' with me. This is some kind of trick—what do you mean, can you ask me questions before you show me the love-letter?!

The older woman says:

If you really knew me, you'd know I'm not the playin' type. Do you know about God-Jesus?

The young woman responds doubtfully:

"Yeah, I heard about him".

The older woman persists gently.

The question was not: Did you hear about Christ Jesus? It was: Do you **know** Him? Do you **know** HIM for yourself?

That's what I'm asking?

The younger woman thinks a little.

Well, let's see, ... I think I heard that God sacrificed His Son for me, and that He departed to prepare a better place. I've heard only Good News about Him.

The older woman smiles, her face lights up. Yes, that's what He is— Good News. But, I'm concerned about the pain written in your face, daughter.

If I can't tell you nothin' else, just remember that **PRAYER CHANGES THINGS,** no matter what is the situation.

Whenever life fails you, God steps in and picks up the pieces—no matter what!

The old woman waits to let this gentle fervor sink in. She talks slowly.

You know, sometimes, we believe more in ourselves than in the one who created us from the beginning. Chile, I tried to **fix my problems.** I was livin' faster than that watch you got on your arm there. But after awhile, I found out that I was creatin' more mess than I could get out of.

I don't want to preach to you—
but would you mind if we had
a moment of prayer? I'll be on my way, after that—
I won't, I'm not pressuring you, no matter what!

The younger woman asks:

Right here?

The older woman smiles.

Yes, right here! I don't have a special place or time to

pray. God say that don't matter. Only thing important is to tell him what you need.

    The younger woman replies.

Well, I guess a few words won't hurt ... I'm in bad enough trouble as it is.

    The younger woman looks at the older woman one smiling.

Give me your hands, daughter! Where-ever there's need, God is. Let's bow our heads.

    From good memory and
    constant habit, she begins to
pray the Prayer of Faith and Healing.

    She is, at first quiet and deliberate, then becomes more fervent.

Our **Father**, we come to You today as two humble children before your Throne. We just want to say, first of all, thank you for wakin' us up this mornin', clothed in our right mind, Father, and with the usage of all the activities of our limbs. Thank you, Lord, for letting us see a brand-new day that we've never seen before for when we were sleepin' through the dangers of the night and totally unconscious of the trouble all around us, **Father**, You protected us. Somebody laid down at the same time we did, **FATHER** but did not rise into this glorious, beautiful, blessed day. I want to thank **you** for all your Goodness and Mercy. This dear sister, Father who was sitting outside with her head hung down in pain, she needs you this evenin', **Father.** I'm asking **you** to stop by this evenin', **Father**—look in on her situation. In Your Word, **Father, you** said that when we seek, we shall find. **You** said that when we knocked, doors would be opened unto us. We standin' at the door. Father, and we knockin'. We need You, **right NOW, FATHER**, to come in and mend broken heart. Create in her, Lord a clean heart and renew in her, **FATHER,** your beautiful spirit. I **know** that through the **BLOOD** You shed that we are able to be healed.

Without, You Father, we're powerless creatures that roam on the earth—we know all Power is in Your Hands. We know you can heal, Father; we know You can deliver. That was **your** promise to us on Calvary.

I'm asking You to give her joy—an unspeakable Joy, Lord, the kind of Joy the world can't take away. I'm asking **you** to fix it for her, **Father.** Fix it, **right now,** that situation in her life. You are the potter, and we are the clay. We **know** you can do all things, because you gave sight to the blind; gave food to the hungry, and made the lame walk. Father, I know the God I serve is an able God, because **one** day, You came into **my** life—and You looked beyond **all**, not just some, but **all** my faults, and still supplied all my needs.
Thank you, God.

Solid As A Rock "I" Stand

I know my God can look beyond the outside of a person, and see on the inside-My God can see the sincereness that rests in the heart.

Father, Oh My Father, the greatest love I've ever known was the love of a Man, who laid down His life for me one day on Calvary when I was yet a sinner.

Since then, I've been carried through life with Grace and Mercy. I ask you to cover this chile with Your blood, Father. Let her walk and not get weary; let her run and not faint; prop her up when she's feelin' lonely, let her feel Your presence. Father, fill every void. Make the crooked places straight—help her climb every mountain, and help her to not linger in the valley. Guide her life, Father, so when she come home to You, **you** can say: "Well done; well done; well done"
Father, we give **you** the praise and the glory. All these blessings we ask in Jesus, Your precious name **AMEN** and **AMEN**.

The younger woman echoes:

"Amen."

The older woman says between sobs:

"Chile, God **is** good, all the time, no matter what! Just like He was good to me, **He'll** be good to you.

The older woman looks penetratingly and gently into the younger woman's eyes.

God loves you all the time, no matter what. I must go, now—but this **Bible** is the **love**-letter that will carry you through the rest of the way. Keep your head up; for God is in the air, and not below your feet. The older woman walks away, putting her handkerchief in her purse. The younger woman intermittently looks after her, and then wipes her uncontrollable tears. She opens the book, and her finger seem to be guided, for they turned to the 27th Psalm and she reads:

THE LORD IS MY LIGHT AND MY SALVATION. WHOM SHALL I FEAR?

Then she turns to Psalm 23rd and reads:

THE LORD IS MY SHEPHERD, I SHALL NOT WANT

She cries some more. A few people pass by; but do not seem to notice her. Suddenly, a glow of light suffuses her face, as she folds her hands to meditate. When she opens her eyes, she returns to another page, which is blank. Suddenly words appear:

I SHALL STILL LOVE THEE, IF THOU WOULD LEAVE THIS MAN, **NO MATTER WHAT!**

Solid As A Rock "I" Stand

GOD AND LUELLA'S CONVERSATION

The True Story of a Man Snatched From The Claws of Death and Other Evils.

I talk with God about some of the unusual people I've known. Here is one of those conversation, recorded from my couch.

I was happy the way things turned out to be, and was asking God to remember the Good Fortune with me.

God: Oh, you mean that young man, Daniel. Well, he was about twenty-seven when he ended that bad marriage. It wasn't one of those weddings made in Heaven, because somehow, thinking they could make big money and get rich quick— for they were poor— the couple decided to sale drugs. At first, they could only make ends meet. But as they became more and more widely known, they money began to pile up in stacks— and they had more than they ever dreamed of. Then one day, on another mistaken idea they thought it was okay to have just any kind of fun, the couple began using what they were selling to others. And it was fun, for awhile. What they didn't know was that things were going downhill; their heads were actually in stormy clouds; not in the fair weather ones they thought they saw.

Solid As A Rock "I" Stand

At first, they thought their marriage had become greater—their sex seemed to be on the hit; and it seemed that they were able to communicate without words. Most drugs always seem to be that kind of "it" the people have always been waiting for.

>Luella: Were you really there all the time?

God: Yes, I was. I remember how he got so into the drug scene that he forgot about his wife, the rent, and only thought about the next high. He never realized that people were passing him by on the street; nor did he seem to care that the police even knew about him. For her part, well, the wife didn't seem to recall much about him either during the later years.

>They had been together since they were teen-agers.

>Luella: Things went from bad to worse.

God: Yes, he became homeless. He said that his shoes were so patched from newspapers that you could, at anytime, catch up with the current events just by looking at his feet. He used to be so important to all his customers, but now he was stealing wallets and purses, shop-lifting, running small-time hustling schemes, even selling his body.

Solid As A Rock "I" Stand

Well, one day, he was just plain unlucky—I say, unlucky for him, but lucky for me. He couldn't find anyone to gang-bang; couldn't find anything to steal from other homeless people; and everyone who walked by with purses looked at him as if to say "don't mess with me" sucker; and no one laid down their purses.

 So he went to one of the few dealers who would still sell him something on a promise of payment, and purchased enough poisonous chemicals to give him the courage to break into someone else's house. It was the thought how frightened the lady might have been who shot him; nor did he care whether there were children, pets, her mother, her father, or anyone one else important living there. But, at last, my work was beginning.

 Weak-kneed, sweating, and with her heart beating wildly, hands shaking, she called the police, thankful, at least, that he didn't want to rape her.

   Luella: Where was the real him?

God: Puffed up in smoke; snorted up in powder; or stuck up in needles.

   Luella: How awful! I'm scared even now just to think about it!

God: I wasn't too pleased about it myself, either.

Luella: What happened? Did life ever began to look up for him?

God: Yes, actually, fortunately for him, they did: All of my best surgeons were on duty. They may not have gone to the top medical schools— I make doctors, too, you know—but they were good with knives and healing needles in that emergency operating room. You may not believe this; but I saw the same specialness in him that—even in those streets—as you saw in him.

But for a while his life was touch-and-go: the bandages, the police questions, the awakening from the hospital and the street drugs. And then, too, Death and Satan were hot on his tail.

Death Angel spoke saying:
God let me have him, let me have him! Oh let me have him!

God: I told them to shut up and go home-even though they were steady screaming: "Let us have him: let us have him."

Then, somehow, a tiny light of understanding must have come to him. Maybe he got it from the nurse's eyes, or in the tone of the policemen's voices, or in the face of the lady's house he broke into.

Solid As A Rock "I" Stand

    Luella: Tell me about the lady,
   again. That's my favorite
part.

God: I covered him with my blood, and both I and My Angels wrapped Our arms around him, and dipped him in the Water of Salvation. Besides that, the lady became so important to him that he wanted to please her. And he wanted to please me, too. And you know, he repented.

    Luella: What? Get out of here!
   He re-re-re-repented!
I said amazingly.

God: He became afraid of what he'd done! He started even doing some little restitution work for those he'd really messed over. I am so proud of him. I want him to be one of my seeds of hope so that others can realize that even they have a possible good future out of a devastated life such as his. Now he knows that I'm never going to walk past him, and that I'm always watching over him. He knows I'm the best homey in the crew.

    Luella: But I've got to ask:
     they're always saying
    in these drug recovery
   programs—once an
addict, always an
  addict. Is that true?

Solid As A Rock "I" Stand

God: You're asking something deep. But I'll give some clues. Being a drug addict is like being a former prisoner or like being handicapped. No matter what you do or how you change, there will always be those people who will never forgive or forget you for what you are or were. You'll always be misunderstood by some and talked about by others. But so what! You simply keep on searching and trying until you find those men and women who are truly your people. Plus, you know that old sticks-and-stones rhyme. So you're not going to let an evil label that you've torn off get stuck back on you again, are you? When I set you free from your errors you are free indeed and I have cast away your old seeds. Pray for strength everyday and I'll hear you and carry you the rest of the way.

 Remember that when you get scared of a mislabeling! ALL WHO ARE IN ME ARE AS NEW CREATURES. And when that happens, you have the power to stand solid as a rock.

 Luella: Thank you, God.

God: Now, don't forget to pray for those who are still lost, including Daniel's first wife. Let's also pray that this new generation is the one to say no everyday to drugs and yes to God everyday.

 Luella: Thank you, God. You're right! Thanks for the reminder.

Solid As A Rock "I" Stand

God: And another thing!

Luella: Yes, God!

God: I'm proud of you; good-night.

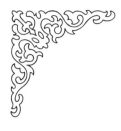

MESSAGE-GRAMS

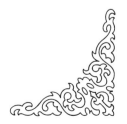

Solid As A Rock "I" Stand

Love is not drawn out on a map;
The wise ones say it just comes in your lap.

Nobody wants to be played like
a baby-grand piano
so don't touch the keyboard
if you can't play fair.

Words that come from the heart of man
leave no empty spaces in the mind.

Solid As A Rock "I" Stand

Adding someone's positive attributes,
then subtracting their negative points
so you can make a decision
=
I can't trust your insight to keep my accounts.

I wonder if anyone knows that
when God put Adam in a deep sleep
and took a rib from his side,
that this symbolizes equality.

When the world throws you out
of its back door,
God welcomes you into the front door.

Solid As A Rock "I" Stand

Luck runs out;
Blessing don't;
Which do you prefer?

Every single day Is my birthday,
because I am re-born in a spiritual way.

When my crib is dirty, it is an apartment;
when clean, it's a suite.

Solid As A Rock "I" Stand

Understanding
+ intelligence
+ Wisdom
and that's progress.

Promises begin as words
and end as actions.

If spaying **RAID** kills cock-roaches,
then what do you think smoking crack does to
people?

Solid As A Rock "I" Stand

Smoking a crack rock
is not the same as standing
on A SOLID ROCK

Gang banging it!?

Always bragging about whose strapped
tighter than who,
keep in mind one of their bullets
may be for you

On Thanksgiving Day,
I always give back to God what he
has given me—
my life in service to others.

Solid As A Rock "I" Stand

Life is like a roller-coaster,
sometimes up and sometimes down.

The next thing you know,
you're all turned around.

Love just won't let me be,
or is it hate?

Not knowing **which** one controls
my destiny leaves me with no peace.

I want peace and joy in my heart;
not someone breaking and stealing just a part.

Solid As A Rock "I" Stand

Human vision is twenty/twenty;
But spiritual vision is sixty/sixty.

Have faith in your creator
for joy will certainly come later.

Faith is certainly the key in impossible times;
Your troubles, however, are not
a challenge to God,
but an opportunity to reveal evidence
of His **power.**

Advertising violence is not
a way of stopping violence.

People come to know violence
by what they see not
by being a minority.

A Natural Degree

We are born with an AA Degree (Almighty Associates Degree) which means you can achieve anything through the one who gave you your first degree for there is no failure in His classroom

Solid As A Rock "I" Stand
Biblical Reference

2 Samuel 22:2

"The Lord is my rock, my fortress, and my deliverer;"

Psalm 27:5

"For in the time of trouble He shall hide me in His pavillion;

In the secret place of His tabernacle
He shall hide me;
He shall set me high
upon a rock."

Psalm 31.3

"For you are my rock
and my fortress;"

Psalm 94:22

"But the Lord has been my defense, and my God is the rock of my refuge."

This book was self published under the direction of Straight From The Heart Associates. For more information on poetry, self-publishing consultation, contact the author, Luella Hill, regarding public readings, consultations, poetry licensing agreements, seminars and workshops at P.O. Box 2208, Oakland, CA 94621.

ORDER FORM

To order additional copies of "Solid As A Rock "I" Stand" or "Black Ties" available from Straight From The Heart Associates, please mail this order form to the address below.

Name _____
Address_____
City _____ State _____ Zip _____

DESCRIPTION	PRICE	QTY	TOTAL
"Solid As A Rock "I" Stand" -Luella Hill	12.95		
"Black Ties" - Danielle Laguerre	15.00		
Subtotal			
CA Residents add 8.25% Sales Tax			
Shipping/Handling: $3.00 + $2.00 each additional item.			
Total			

PAYMENT

Send a copy of this order form with a Check or Money Order payable to Straight From The Heart Associates.

Straight From The Heart Associates
P.O. Box 2208
Oakland, CA 94621

Please allow 4-6 weeks for delivery